TO:

FROM:

DATE:

Majestic Expressions
Savage, Minnesota, USA

Majestic Expressions is an imprint of BroadStreet Publishing Group, LLC.
Broadstreetpublishing.com

God's Words for You

9781424565757

Typesetting and design by Garborg Design Works | garborgdesign.com
Editorial services by Michelle Winger | literallyprecise.com

Printed in China.

24 25 26 27 28 29 30   7 6 5 4 3 2 1

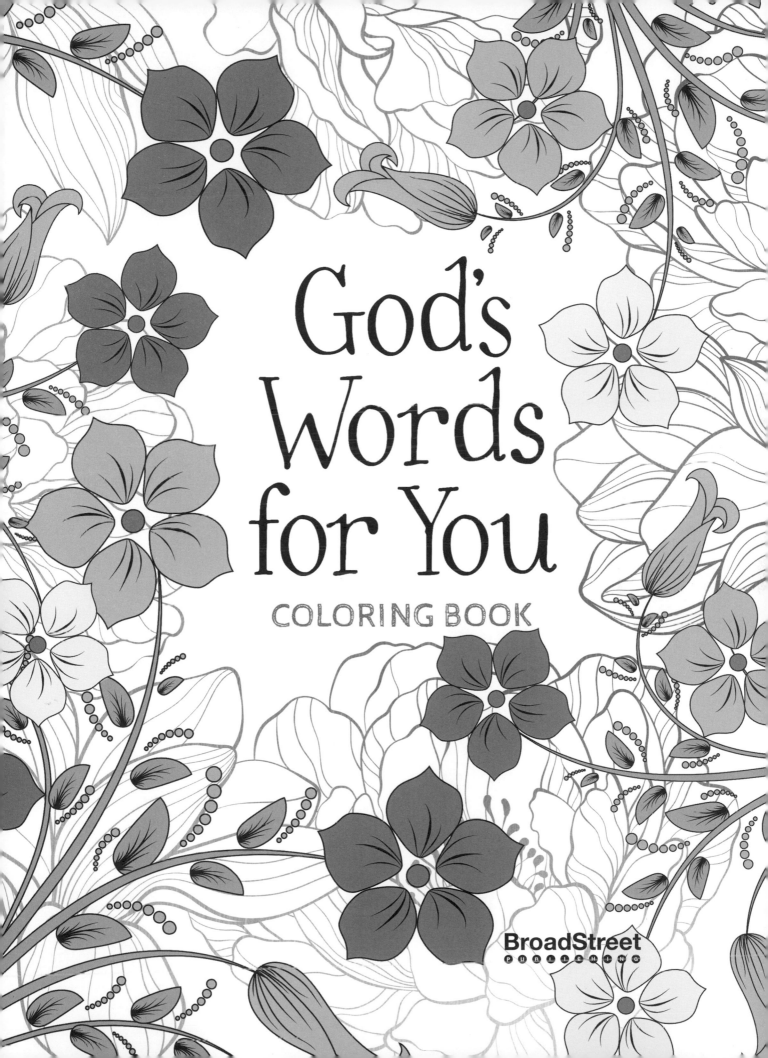

God's Words for You

COLORING BOOK

BroadStreet
PUBLISHING

When your
faith is tested,
your endurance
has a chance
to grow.

JAMES 1:3 NLT

You, O Lord, are **good** and forgiving, abounding in **steadfast love** to all who call upon you.

PSALM 86:5 ESV

My people, who bear my name, humble themselves, pray and
seek my face, and turn from their evil ways, then I will hear from
heaven, forgive their sin, and heal their land.

2 CHRONICLES 7:14 CSB

THE
PEACE
OF GOD,
WHICH SURPASSES ALL
COMPREHENSION, WILL GUARD
YOUR HEARTS AND MINDS
IN CHRIST JESUS.
PHILIPPIANS 4:7 NASB

In this world
you will have
trouble. But
take heart!
I have overcome
the world.

JOHN 16:33 NIV

This
is what
the Son
promised to us—
life forever.

1 JOHN 2:25 NCV

Do not fear,
for I am
with you.

ISAIAH 41:10 NIV

Even when
I have trouble
all around me,
you will keep
me alive.

PSALM 138:7 NCV

THE LORD
IS MY LIGHT
AND MY
SALVATION;
WHOM
SHALL I
FEAR?

PSALM 27:1 ESV

You will keep in perfect peace those whose minds are steadfast because they trust in you.

ISAIAH 26:3 NIV

GOD CAUSES EVERYTHING TO WORK TOGETHER FOR THE GOOD OF THOSE WHO LOVE GOD.

ROMANS 8:28 NLT

Blessed are those who mourn, for they will be comforted.

MATTHEW 5:4 NIV

The LORD himself goes before you and will be with you; he will not leave you nor forsake you.

DEUTERONOMY 31:8 NIV

I am
making
everything
new.

REVELATION 21:5 NCV

I WILL INSTRUCT YOU AND TEACH YOU IN THE WAY YOU SHOULD GO.

PSALM 32:8 NIV

GOD ALWAYS DOES WHAT IS RIGHT AND FAIR.

ROMANS 3:25 NCV

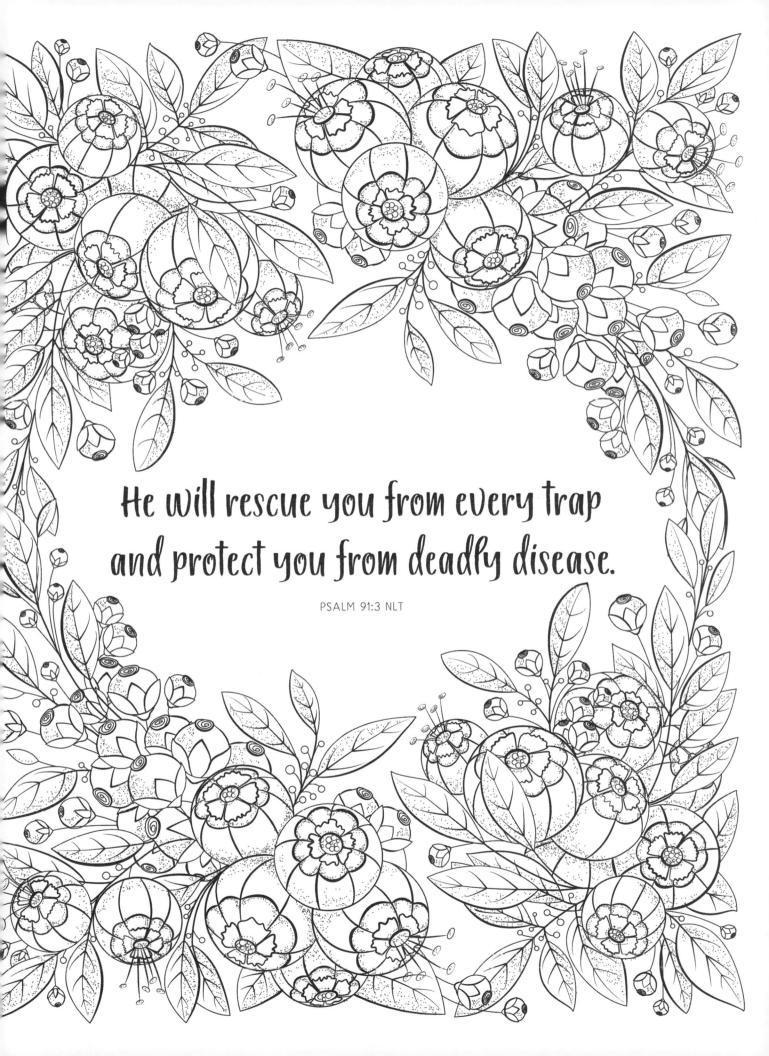

He will rescue you from every trap
and protect you from deadly disease.

PSALM 91:3 NLT

God loves a cheerful giver.

2 CORINTHIANS 9:7 CSB

Come to me,
all you who
are weary
and burdened,
and I will
give you rest.

MATTHEW 11:28 NIV

By his
wounds,
you have
been healed.

1 PETER 2:24 NIV

He gives power to the weak and strength to the powerless.

ISAIAH 40:29 NLT

Blessed are the pure in heart, for they will see God.

MATTHEW 5:8 NIV

For I know the plans I have for you... to give you a future and a hope.

JEREMIAH 29:11 NLT

I am about to do something new; even now it is coming.

ISAIAH 43:19 CSB

I will fear
no evil,
for you are
with me.

PSALM 23:4 ESV

The mountains may move and the hills disappear,

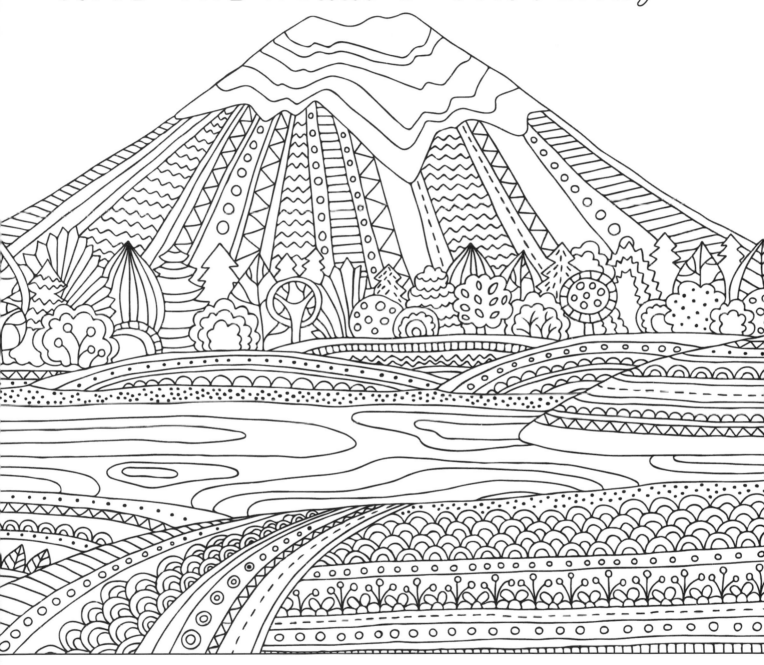

But even then my faithful love for you will remain.

ISAIAH 54:10 NLT

If you confess with your mouth Jesus as Lord, and believe in your heart that God raised Him from the dead, you will be saved.

ROMANS 10:9 NASB

Delight

yourself in the Lord,
and he will give you the
desires of your heart.

PSALM 37:4 ESV

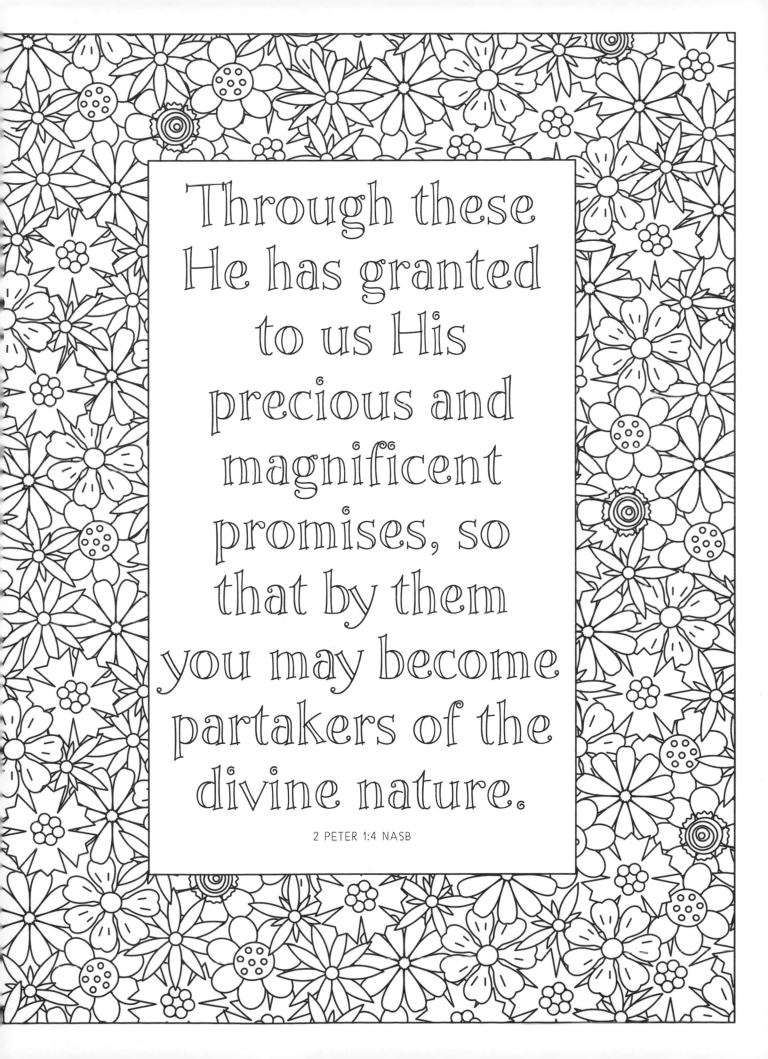

Through these He has granted to us His precious and magnificent promises, so that by them you may become partakers of the divine nature.

2 PETER 1:4 NASB

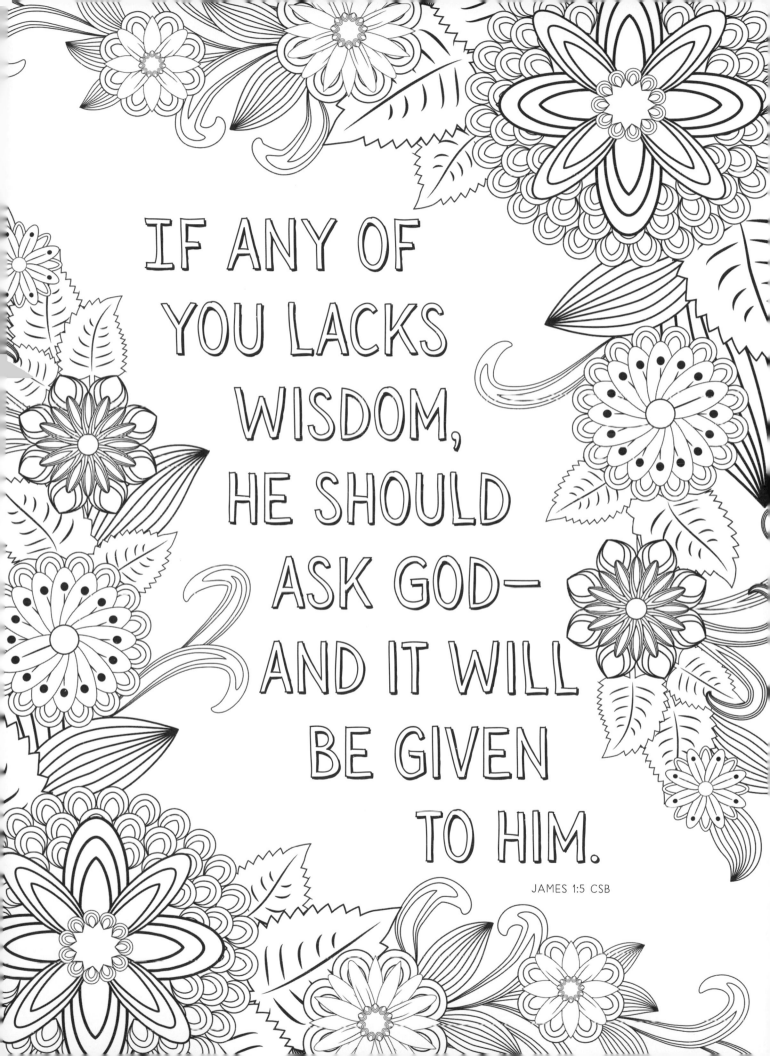

IF ANY OF YOU LACKS WISDOM, HE SHOULD ASK GOD— AND IT WILL BE GIVEN TO HIM.

JAMES 1:5 CSB

Come close to God, and God will come close to you.

JAMES 4:8 NLT

When the righteous cry for help, the LORD hears and delivers them out of all their troubles.

PSALM 34:17 ESV

You will seek me and find me when you seek me with all your heart.

JEREMIAH 29:13 NIV

Blessed are the merciful,
for they will be shown mercy.

MATTHEW 5:7 NIV

See if I will not open the floodgates of heaven and pour out a blessing for you without measure.

MALACHI 3:10 CSB

GOD WILL SUPPLY EVERY NEED OF YOURS ACCORDING TO HIS RICHES IN GLORY IN CHRIST JESUS. PHILIPPIANS 4:19 ESV

He has sent me to heal the brokenhearted,
to proclaim liberty to the captives
and freedom to the prisoners.

ISAIAH 61:1 CSB

Seek first his kingdom
and his righteousness,
and all these things will
be given to you as well.

MATTHEW 6:33 NIV

MY GRACE IS
SUFFICIENT FOR YOU,
FOR MY POWER IS
MADE PERFECT
IN WEAKNESS.

2 CORINTHIANS 12:9 NIV

Ask, and God will give to you. Search, and you will find. Knock, and the door will open for you.

MATTHEW 7:7 NCV

If the *Son* sets you free, you really will be free.

JOHN 8:36 CSB

YOU WILL RECEIVE YOUR REWARD FROM THE LORD, WHICH HE PROMISED TO HIS PEOPLE.

COLOSSIANS 3:24 NCV

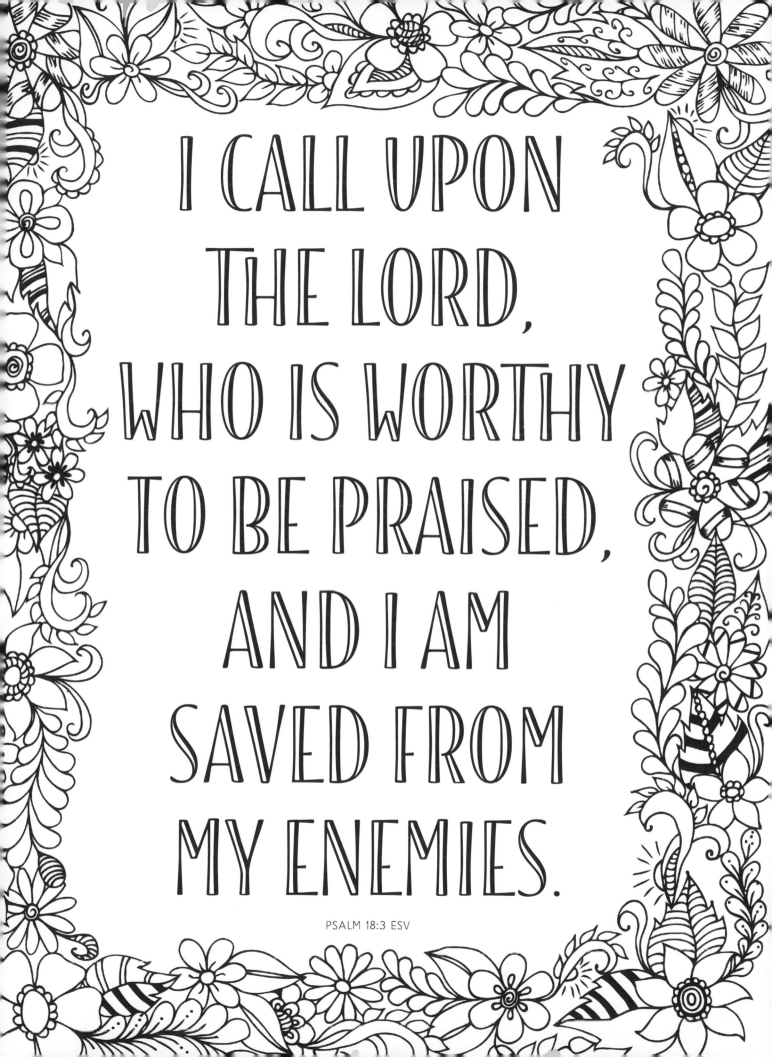

I CALL UPON THE LORD, WHO IS WORTHY TO BE PRAISED, AND I AM SAVED FROM MY ENEMIES.

PSALM 18:3 ESV

NO WEAPON FORMED AGAINST YOU WILL SUCCEED.

ISAIAH 54:17 CSB

Be strong and courageous...for the Lord your God is with you wherever you go.

JOSHUA 1:9 ESV

The one who
believes in
the Son has
eternal life.

JOHN 3:36 CSB

LET YOUR REQUESTS BE MADE KNOWN TO GOD.

PHILIPPIANS 4:6 NASB

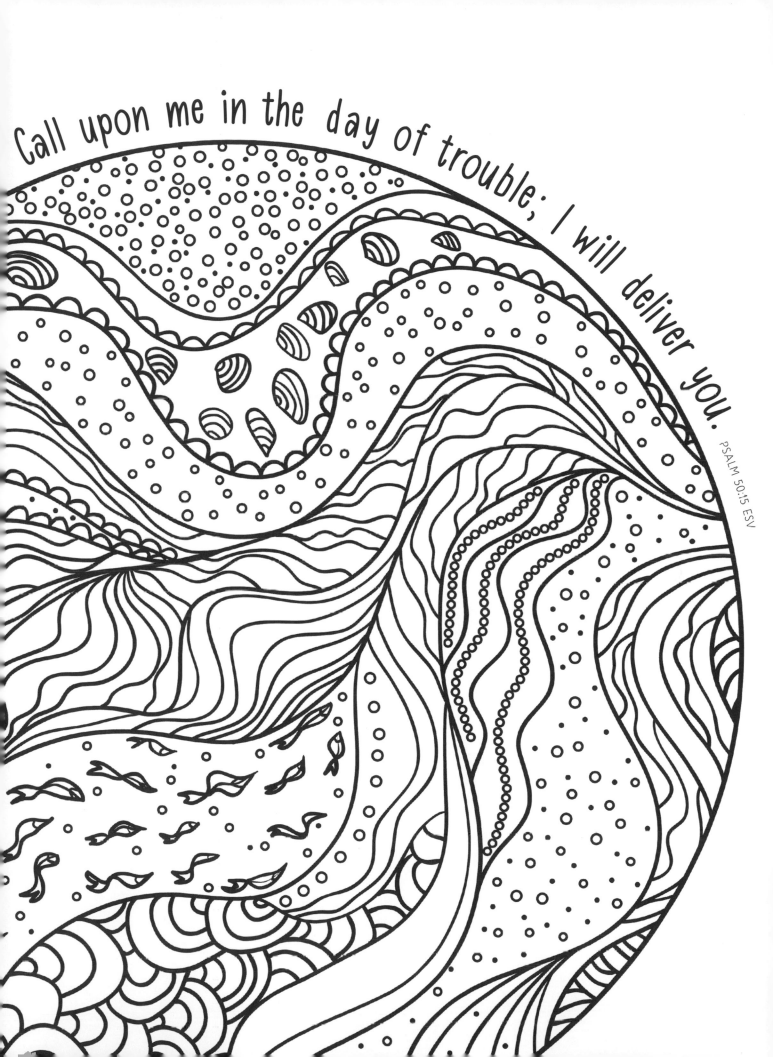

Call upon me in the day of trouble; I will deliver you. PSALM 50:15 ESV

If we confess our sins, he is faithful and righteous to forgive us our sins and to cleanse us from all unrighteousness.

1 JOHN 1:9 CSB

The Lord
makes firm the
steps of the one
who delights in him.

PSALM 37:23 NIV

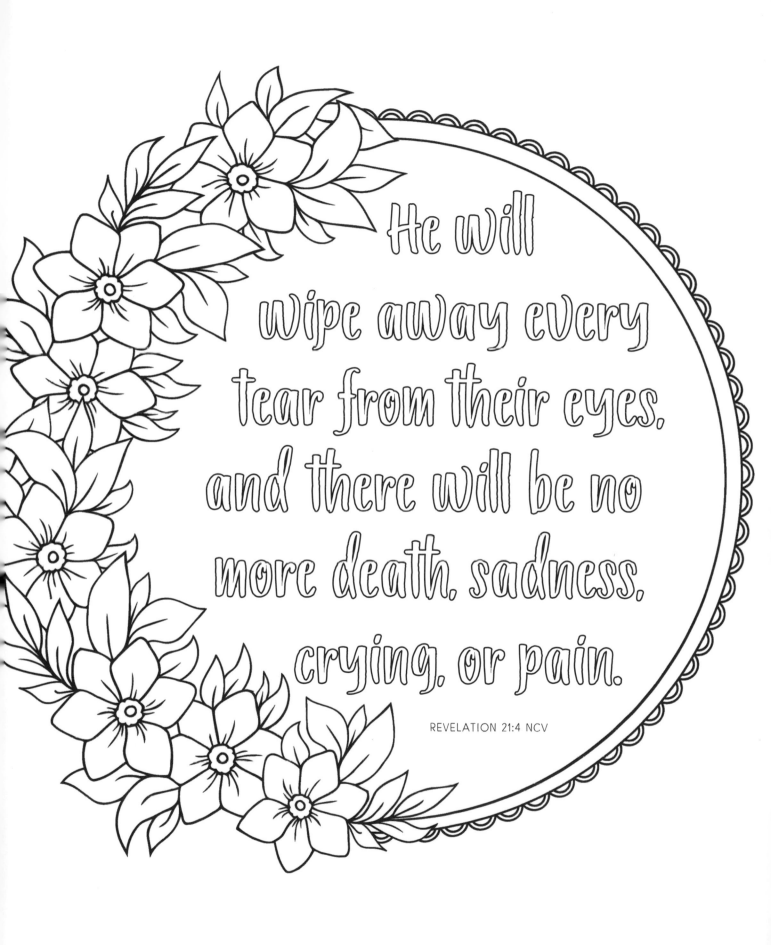

He will wipe away every tear from their eyes, and there will be no more death, sadness, crying, or pain.

REVELATION 21:4 NCV

I hold you by your right hand.

ISAIAH 41:13 NLT

You, LORD, have not abandoned those who seek You.

PSALM 9:10 NASB

The LORD reproves him whom he loves.

PROVERBS 3:12 ESV

When you go through rivers of difficulty, you will not drown.

ISAIAH 43:2 NLT

In all your ways
acknowledge Him,
And He will
make your
paths straight.

PROVERBS 3:6 NASB

HE GAVE HIS
ONE AND ONLY
SON, SO THAT
EVERYONE
WHO BELIEVES
IN HIM WILL
NOT PERISH
BUT HAVE
ETERNAL LIFE.

JOHN 3:16 CSB

Submit to God. Resist the devil, and he will flee from you.

JAMES 4:7 CSB

The LORD himself will fight for you. Just stay calm.

EXODUS 14:14 NLT

Whatever you ask in prayer, believe that you have received it, and it will be yours.

MARK 11:24 ESV

The water I give them will become
in them a spring of water
welling up to eternal life.

JOHN 4:14 NIV

SEEK FIRST HIS KINGDOM
AND HIS RIGHTEOUSNESS,
AND ALL THESE THINGS WILL
BE GIVEN TO YOU AS WELL.

MATTHEW 6:33 NIV